Helen Steiner Rice

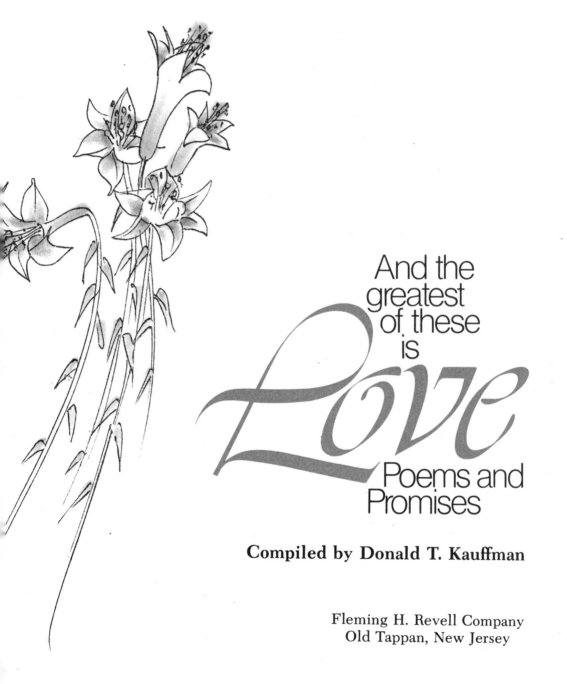

And the greatest of these is Love

Poems and Promises

Compiled by Donald T. Kauffman

Fleming H. Revell Company
Old Tappan, New Jersey

Unless otherwise indicated, Scripture quotations are from the King James Version of the Bible.

Scripture quotations identified RSV are from the Revised Standard Version of the Bible, copyrighted 1946, 1952, © 1971 and 1973.

Scripture quotations identified NEB are from The New English Bible. © The Delegates of the Oxford University Press and the Syndics of the Cambridge University Press 1961 and 1970. Reprinted by permission.

Book design and illustrations by John Okladek.

Library of Congress Cataloging in Publication Data

Rice, Helen Steiner
  Love.

  I. Title.
PS3568.I28L55   811'.5'4   79-19264
ISBN 0-8007-1072-X
ISBN 0-8007-1073-8 keepsake ed.

Presented to :

Arlene Girrens

From :

with love

Duane + Judy Thome

By Helen Steiner Rice

Heart Gifts From Helen Steiner Rice
Lovingly, Helen Steiner Rice
Prayerfully
Someone Cares
The Story of the Christmas Guest
Life Is Forever
Loving Promises
A Gift of Love
Everyone Needs Someone
Somebody Loves You
Love

Contents

Preface

". . . and the greatest of these is LOVE." How true this is today!

The one thing most needed by everyone is real, caring love. And the Source of all love is God, who *is* Love. His love is available for all of us, but we need to learn to love each other. We are all lonely but we are never alone, for God is our Father and we are His own.

My verses come to me from the thoughts and feelings of people who write to me, or from conversations I have. They beat to the pulse of Love: theirs and His. I know I cannot make it on my own, so I ask God to take my hand and hold it tight, for I cannot walk alone.

I am very pleased that my friend Donald Kauffman has arranged these verses, with appropriate quotations from Scripture to carry the message of love. We always need to remember the Father's love. And the words that never fail us are the words of God above.

These are words to help you remember ideas that never grow old—perhaps in new ways. My constant reliance on God enables me to bring these words together with the hope that you may find renewed faith and the blessing of God's love.

HELEN STEINER RICE

And the
greatest
of these
is
Love

Thank God for Little Things

Thank you, God, for little things
      that often come our way—
The things we take for granted
      but don't mention when we pray—
The unexpected courtesy,
      the thoughtful, kindly deed—
A hand reached out to help us
      in the time of sudden need—
Oh, make us more aware, dear God,
      of little daily graces
That come to us with "sweet surprise"
      from never-dreamed-of places.

Blessed be the Lord,
  who daily loadeth us with benefits . . . .
                        Psalms 68:19

"Climb 'Til Your Dream Comes True"

Often your tasks will be many,
And more than you think you can do . . .
Often the road will be rugged
And the hills insurmountable, too . . .
But always remember, the hills ahead
Are never as steep as they seem,
And with *Faith* in your heart start upward
And climb 'til you reach your dream,
For nothing in life that is worthy
Is ever too hard to achieve
If you have the courage to try it
And you have the *Faith* to believe . . .
For *Faith* is a force that is greater
Than knowledge or power or skill
And many defeats turn to triumph
If you trust in God's wisdom and will . . .
For Faith is a mover of mountains,
There's nothing that God cannot do,
So start out today with Faith in your heart
And *"Climb 'Til Your Dreams Come True"!*

. . . If thou canst believe,
all things are possible to him that believeth.

Mark 9:23

12

Showers of Blessings

Each day there are showers of blessings
     sent from the Father Above,
For God is a great, lavish giver
     and there is no end to His love—
His grace is more than sufficient,
     His mercy is boundless and deep,
And His infinite blessings are countless
     and all this we're given to keep,
If we but seek God and find Him
     and ask for a bounteous measure
Of this wholly immeasurable offering
     from God's inexhaustible treasure—
For no matter how big man's dreams are,
     God's blessings are Infinitely more,
For always God's Giving is greater
     than what man is Asking for.

Ask, and it shall be given you;
   seek, and ye shall find;
     knock, and it shall be opened unto you.
If ye then, being evil,
   know how to give good gifts unto your children,
     how much more shall your Father which is in heaven
       give good things to them that ask him?
                 Matthew 7:7, 11

There's Sunshine
in a Smile

Life is a mixture
        of sunshine and rain,
Laughter and pleasure,
        teardrops and pain,
All days can't be bright,
        but it's certainly true,
There was never a cloud
        the sun didn't shine through—
So just keep on smiling
        whatever betide you,
Secure in the knowledge
        God is always beside you,
And you'll find when you smile
        your day will be brighter
And all of your burdens
        will seem so much lighter—
For each time you smile
        you will find it's true
Somebody, somewhere
        will *smile back at you,*
And nothing on earth
        can make life more worthwhile
Than the sunshine and warmth
        of a *beautiful smile.*

   . . . for he maketh his sun to rise on the evil and on the good,
and sendeth rain on the just and on the unjust.
   Be ye therefore perfect, even as your Father which is in
heaven is perfect.

Matthew 5:45, 48

God's Tender Care

When trouble comes,
    as it does to us all
God is so great
    and we are so small—
But there is nothing
    that we need know
If we have faith
    that wherever we go
God will be waiting
    to help us bear
Our pain and sorrow,
    our suffering and care—
For no pain or suffering
    is ever too much
To yield itself
    to God's merciful touch!

**The Lord is gracious, and
full of compassion; slow to anger,
and of great mercy.
The Lord is good to all:
and his tender mercies are
over all his works.**

                Psalms 145:8, 9

Quit Supposin'

Don't start your day by supposin'
    that trouble is just ahead,
It's better to stop supposin'
    and start with a prayer instead,
And make it a prayer of *Thanksgiving*
    for the wonderful things God has wrought
Like the beautiful sunrise and sunset,
    "God's Gifts" that are free and not bought—
For what is the use of supposin'
    the dire things that could happen to you
And worry about some misfortune
    that seldom if ever comes true—
But instead of just idle supposin'
    step forward to meet each new day
Secure in the knowledge God's near you
    to lead you each step of the way—
For supposin' the worst things will happen
    only helps to make them come true
And you darken the bright, happy moments
    that the dear Lord has given to you—
So if you desire to be happy
    and get rid of the *"misery* of *dread"*
Just give up *"Supposin' the worst things"*
    and look for *"the best things"* instead.

For as he thinketh in his heart, so is he . . . .
Proverbs 23:7

Anywhere Is a Place of Prayer
if God Is There

I have prayed on my knees in the morning,
I have prayed as I walked along,
I have prayed in the silence and darkness
And I've prayed to the tune of a song—
I have prayed in the midst of triumph
And I've prayed when I suffered defeat,
I have prayed on the sands of the seashore
Where the waves of the ocean beat—
I have prayed in a velvet-hushed forest
Where the quietness calmed my fears,
I have prayed through suffering and heartache
When my eyes were blinded with tears—
I have prayed in churches and chapels,
Cathedrals and synagogues, too,
But often I've had the feeling
That my prayers were not getting through,
And I realized then that our Father
Is not really concerned where we pray
Or impressed by our manner of worship
Or the eloquent words we say . . .
He is only concerned with our feelings,
And He looks deep into our heart
And hears the "cry of our soul's deep need"
That no words could ever impart . . .
So it isn't the prayer that's expressive
Or offered in some special spot,
It's the sincere plea of a sinner
And God can tell whether or not
We honestly seek His forgiveness
And earnestly mean what we say,
And then and then only He answers
The prayer that we fervently pray.

**. . . The effectual fervent prayer of a righteous man availeth
much.**

James 5:16

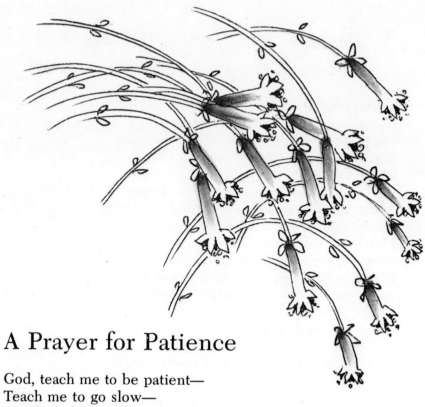

A Prayer for Patience

God, teach me to be patient—
Teach me to go slow—
Teach me how to "wait on You"
When my way I do not know . . .
Teach me sweet forbearance
When things do not go right
So I remained unruffled
When others grow uptight . . .
Teach me how to quiet
My racing, rising heart
So I may hear the answer
You are trying to impart . . .
Teach me to LET GO, dear God,
And pray undisturbed until
My heart is filled with inner peace
And I learn to know YOUR WILL!

Be still, and know that I am God . . . .
                                    Psalms 46:10

Nothing on Earth Is Forever Yours— Only the Love of the Lord Endures!

Everything in life is passing
    and whatever we possess
Cannot endure forever
    but ends in nothingness,
For there are no safety boxes
    nor vaults that can contain
The possessions we collected
    and desire to retain . . .
So all that man acquires,
    be it power, fame or jewels,
Is but limited and earthly,
    only "treasure made for fools" . . .
For only in GOD'S KINGDOM
    can man find enduring treasure,
Priceless gifts of love and beauty—
    more than mortal man can measure,
And the "riches" he accumulates
    he can keep and part with never,
For only in GOD'S KINGDOM
    do our treasures last FOREVER . . .
So use the word FOREVER
    with sanctity and love,
For NOTHING IS FOREVER
    BUT THE LOVE OF GOD ABOVE!

O give thanks unto the Lord;
    for he is good:
        for his mercy endureth for ever.
                Psalms 136:1

There's Peace and Calm in the Twenty-Third Psalm

With THE LORD as "YOUR SHEPHERD"
     you have all that you need,
For, if you "FOLLOW IN HIS FOOTSTEPS"
     wherever HE may lead,
HE will guard and guide and keep you
     in HIS loving, watchful care
And, when traveling in "dark valleys,"
     "YOUR SHEPHERD" will be there . . .
HIS goodness is unfailing,
     HIS kindness knows no end,
For THE LORD is a "GOOD SHEPHERD"
     on whom you can depend . . .
So, when your heart is troubled,
     you'll find quiet peace and calm
If you'll open up the Bible
     and just read this treasured Psalm.

The Lord is my shepherd; I shall not want. He maketh me to lie down in green pastures: he leadeth me beside the still waters. He restoreth my soul: he leadeth me in the paths of righteousness for his name's sake. Yea, though I walk through the valley of the shadow of death, I will fear no evil: for thou art with me; thy rod and thy staff they comfort me. Thou preparest a table before me in the presence of mine enemies: thou anointest my head with oil; my cup runneth over. Surely goodness and mercy shall follow me all the days of my life: and I will dwell in the house of the Lord for ever.

Psalm 23

The Better You Know Him, the More You Love Him!

The better you know GOD, the better you feel,
For to learn more about HIM and discover HE'S REAL
Can wholly, completely and miraculously change,
Reshape and remake and then rearrange
Your mixed-up, miserable and unhappy life
"Adrift on the sea of sin-sickened strife"—
But when you once know this "MAN of GOOD WILL,"
HE will calm your life and say "PEACE, BE STILL" . . .
So open your "heart's door" and let CHRIST come in
And HE'LL give you new life and free you from sin—
And there is no joy that can ever compare
With the joy of knowing you're in GOD'S care.

**. . . God is love;
and he that dwelleth in love dwelleth in God,
and God in him.**

1 John 4:16

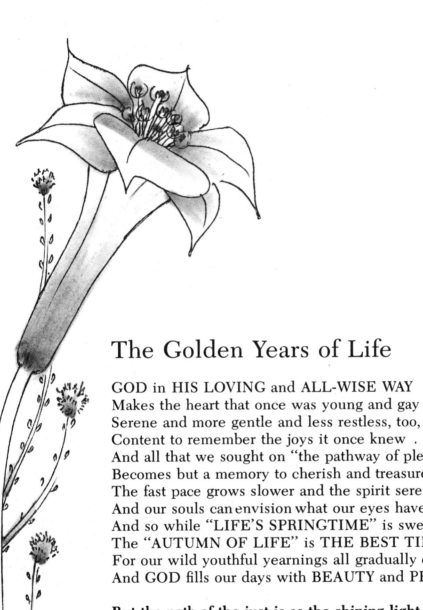

The Golden Years of Life

GOD in HIS LOVING and ALL-WISE WAY
Makes the heart that once was young and gay
Serene and more gentle and less restless, too,
Content to remember the joys it once knew . . .
And all that we sought on "the pathway of pleasure"
Becomes but a memory to cherish and treasure—
The fast pace grows slower and the spirit serene,
And our souls can envision what our eyes have not seen . . .
And so while "LIFE'S SPRINGTIME" is sweet to recall,
The "AUTUMN OF LIFE" is THE BEST TIME of all,
For our wild youthful yearnings all gradually cease
And GOD fills our days with BEAUTY and PEACE!

But the path of the just is as the shining light,
  that shineth more and more unto the perfect day.
                                        Proverbs 4:18

God's Love

GOD'S LOVE is like an island
In life's ocean vast and wide—
A peaceful, quiet shelter
From the restless, rising tide . . .

GOD'S LOVE is like an anchor
When the angry billows roll—
A mooring in the storms of life,
A stronghold for the soul . . .

GOD'S LOVE is like a fortress
And we seek protection there
When the waves of tribulation
Seem to drown us in despair . . .

GOD'S LOVE is like a harbor
Where our souls can find sweet rest
From the struggle and the tension
Of life's fast and futile quest . . .

GOD'S LOVE is like a beacon
Burning bright with FAITH and PRAYER
And through the changing scenes of life
We can find a HAVEN THERE!

Oh how great is thy goodness,
  which thou hast laid up for them that fear thee;
which thou hast wrought for them that trust in thee
  before the sons of men!
Be of good courage, and he shall strengthen your heart,
  all ye that hope in the Lord.
                                          Psalms 31:19, 24

The Praying Hands

The *"Praying Hands"* are much, much more
    than just a work of art,
They are the "soul's creation"
    of a deeply thankful heart—
They are a *Priceless Masterpiece*
    that love alone could paint,
And they reveal the selflessness
    of an unheralded saint—
These hands so scarred and toilworn,
    tell the story of a man
Who sacrificed his talent
    in accordance with God's plan—
For in God's Plan are many things
    man cannot understand,
But we must trust God's judgment
    and be guided by His Hand—
Sometimes He asks us to give up
    our dreams of happiness,
Sometimes we must forego our hopes
    of fortune and success,
Not all of us can triumph
    or rise to heights of fame,
And many times *What Should Be Ours,*
    goes to *Another Name*—
But he who makes a sacrifice,
    so another may succeed,
Is indeed a true disciple
    of our blessed Saviour's creed—
For when we "give ourselves away"
    in sacrifice and love,
We are "laying up rich treasures"
    in God's kingdom up above—
And hidden in gnarled, toilworn hands
    is the truest *Art of Living,*
Achieved alone by those who've learned
    the *"Victory of Giving"*—
For any sacrifice on earth
    made in the dear Lord's name,

Assures the giver of a place
        in *Heaven's Hall of Fame*—
And who can say with certainty
        Where *The Greatest Talent Lies,*
Or Who Will Be The Greatest
        In Our Heavenly Father's Eyes!
And who can tell with certainty
        in the heavenly *Father's Sight*
Who's entitled to the *"medals"*
        And who's the *"hero of the fight."*

But lay up for yourselves treasures in heaven . . .
                                Matthew 6:20

29

Blessings Come in Many Guises

When troubles come
        and things go wrong,
And days are cheerless
        and nights are long,
We find it so easy
        to give in to despair
By magnifying
        the burdens we bear—
We add to our worries
        by refusing to try
To look for "the rainbow"
        in an overcast sky—
And the blessing God sent
        in a "darkened disguise"
Our troubled hearts
        fail to recognize,
Not knowing God sent it
        not to distress us
But to strengthen our faith
        and redeem us and bless us.

Humble yourselves therefore under the mighty hand of God,
that he may exalt you in due time;
Casting all your care upon him: for he careth for you.

1 Peter 5:6, 7

God, Are You Really Real?

I want to believe
I want to be true
I want to be loyal
And faithful to YOU.
But where can I go
When vague doubts arise
And when "EVIL" appears
In an "ANGEL'S DISGUISE"
While clamoring voices
Demand my attention
And the air is polluted
With cries of dissension,
You know, God, it's easy
Just to follow the crowd
Who are "doing their thing"
While shouting out loud
Gross protestations
Against the "old rules"
That limit and hamper
The NEW FREEDOM SCHOOLS . . .
God, answer this prayer
And tell me the truth
Are YOU really the God
Of both Age and of Youth?
And, God, speak to my heart
So I truly feel
That "these prophets" are false
But YOU REALLY ARE REAL!

God Knows Best

Our Father knows what's best for us,
So why should we complain—
We always want the sunshine,
But He knows there must be rain—
We love the sound of laughter
And the merriment of cheer,
But our hearts would lose their tenderness
If we never shed a tear . . .
Our Father tests us often
With suffering and with sorrow,
He tests us, not to punish us,
But to help us meet TOMORROW . . .
For growing trees are strengthened
When they withstand the storm,
And the sharp cut of the chisel
Gives the marble grace and form . . .
God never hurts us needlessly,
And He never wastes our pain,
For every loss He sends to us
Is followed by rich gain . . .
And when we count the blessings
That God has so freely sent,
We will find no cause for murmuring
And no time to lament . . .
For Our Father loves His children,
And to Him all things are plain,
So He never sends us PLEASURE
When the SOUL'S DEEP NEED IS PAIN . . .
So whenever we are troubled,
And when everything goes wrong,
It is just God working in us
To make OUR SPIRIT STRONG.

Wherefore let them that suffer according to the will of God commit the keeping of their souls to him in well doing, as unto a faithful Creator.

1 Peter 4:19

Everywhere Across the Land You See God's Face and Touch His Hand

Each time you look up in the sky
Or watch the fluffy clouds drift by,
Or feel the sunshine warm and bright,
Or watch the dark night turn to light,
Or hear a bluebird gayly sing,
Or see the winter turn to spring,
Or stop to pick a daffodil,
Or gather violets on some hill . . .
Or touch a leaf or see a tree,
It's all *God* whispering *"This is Me . . .*
And *I* am *Faith* and *I* am *Light*
And *in Me there shall be no night."*

For in him we live, and move, and have our being . . . .
Acts 17:28

God's Stairway

Step by step we climb each day
Closer to God with each prayer we pray
For "the cry of the heart" offered in prayer
Becomes just another "SPIRITUAL STAIR"
In the "HEAVENLY STAIRCASE" leading us to
A beautiful place where we live anew . . .
So never give up for it's worth the climb
To live forever in "ENDLESS TIME"
Where the soul of man is SAFE and FREE
To LIVE IN LOVE THROUGH ETERNITY!

. . . but he that doeth the will of God abideth for ever.
1 John 2:17

For One Who Gives So Much to Others

It's not the things that can be bought
    that are life's richest treasure,
It's just the little "heart gifts"
    that money cannot measure . . .
A cheerful smile, a friendly word,
    a sympathetic nod
Are priceless little treasures
    from the storehouse of our God . . .
They are the things that can't be bought
    with silver or with gold,
For thoughtfulness and kindness
    and love are never sold . . .
They are the priceless things in life
    for which no one can pay,
And the giver finds rich recompense
    in *Giving Them Away*.
And who on earth gives more away
    and does more good for others
Than understanding, kind and wise
    and selfless, loving *Mothers*
Who ask no more than just the joy
    of helping those they love
To find in life the happiness
    that they are dreaming of.

God, Grant Me the Glory of "Thy Gift"

God, widen my vision so I may see
     the afflictions You have sent to me—
Not as a CROSS too heavy to bear
     that weighs me down in gloomy despair—
Not as something to hate and despise
     but a GIFT of LOVE sent in disguise—
Something to draw me closer to You
     to teach me PATIENCE and FORBEARANCE, too—
Something to show me more clearly the way
     to SERVE You and LOVE You more every day—
Something PRICELESS and PRECIOUS and RARE
     that will keep me forever SAFE in Thy CARE
Aware of the SPIRITUAL STRENGTH that is mine
     if my selfish, small will is lost in Thine!

   . . . Let us exult in the hope of the divine splendour that is to be ours. More than this: let us even exult in our present sufferings, because we know that suffering trains us to endure, and endurance brings proof that we have stood the test, and this proof is the ground of hope. Such a hope is no mockery, because God's love has flooded our inmost heart through the Holy Spirit he has given us.

Romans 5:2–5 (NEB)

If You Meet God in the Morning, He'll Go With You Through the Day

"The earth is the Lord's
    and the fulness thereof"—
It speaks of His greatness,
    it sings of His love,
And each day at dawning
    I lift my heart high
And raise up my eyes
    to the infinite sky . . .
I watch the night vanish
    as a new day is born,
And I hear the bird's song
    on the wings of the morn,
I see the dew glisten
    in crystal-like splendor
While God, with a touch
    that is gentle and tender,
Wraps up the night
    and softly tucks it away
And hangs out the sun
    to herald a new day . . .
And so I give thanks
    and my heart kneels to pray—
"God keep me and guide me
    and go with me today."

Every day will I bless thee;
    and I will praise thy name for ever and ever.
Great is the Lord, and greatly to be praised;
    and his greatness is unsearchable.
The Lord is gracious, and full of compassion;
    slow to anger, and of great mercy.
The Lord is good to all:
    and his tender mercies are over all his works.
Psalms 145:2, 3, 8, 9

In Hours of Discouragement God Is Our Encouragement

Sometimes we feel uncertain
And unsure of everything,
Afraid to make decisions,
Dreading what the day will bring—
We keep wishing it were possible
To dispel all fear and doubt
And to understand more readily
Just what life is all about—
God has given us the answers
Which too often go unheeded,
But if we search His promises
We'll find everything that's needed
To lift our faltering spirits
And renew our courage, too,
For there's absolutely nothing
Too much for God to do—
For the Lord is our salvation
And our strength in every fight,
Our redeemer and protector,
Our eternal guiding light—
He has promised to sustain us,
He's our refuge from all harms,
And underneath this refuge,
Are the everlasting arms—
So cast your burden on Him,
Seek His counsel when distressed,
And go to Him for comfort
When you're lonely and oppressed—
For God is our encouragement
In trouble and in trials,
And in suffering and in sorrow
He will turn our tears to smiles.

He giveth power to the faint;
    and to them that have no might he increaseth strength.
Even the youths shall faint and be weary,
    and the young men shall utterly fall:
        But they that wait upon the Lord shall renew their strength;
        they shall mount up with wings as eagles;
           they shall run, and not be weary;
           and they shall walk, and not faint.

                          Isaiah 40:29–31

God's Jewels

We watch the rich and famous
Bedecked in precious jewels,
Enjoying earthly pleasures,
Defying moral rules—
And in our mood of discontent
We sink into despair
And long for earthly riches
And feel cheated of our share—
But stop these idle musings,
God has stored up for you
Treasures that are far beyond
Earth's jewels and riches, too—
For never, never discount
What God has promised man
If he will walk in meekness
And accept God's flawless plan—
For if we heed His teachings
As we journey through the years,
We'll find the richest jewels of all
Are *crystallized* from *tears.*

Because thy lovingkindness is better than life,
  my lips shall praise thee.
Thus will I bless thee while I live:
  I will lift up my hands in thy name.
Because thou hast been my help,
  therefore in the shadow of thy wings will I rejoice.
                                    Psalms 63:3, 4, 7

It's a Wonderful World

In spite of the fact
    we complain and lament
And view this old world
    with much discontent,
Deploring conditions
    and grumbling because
There's so much injustice
    and so many flaws,
It's a wonderful world
    and it's people like you
Who make it that way
    by the things that they do—
For a warm, ready smile
    or a kind, thoughtful deed,
Or a hand outstretched
    in an hour of need
Can change our whole outlook
    and make the world bright
Where a minute before
    just nothing seemed right—
It's a Wonderful World
    and it always will be
If we keep our eyes open
    and focused to see
The Wonderful Things
    man is capable of
When he opens his heart
    to God and His love.

**The earth is the Lord's, and
the fulness thereof; the world,
and they that dwell therein.**
Psalms 24:1

The Joy of Unselfish Giving

Time is not measured
     by the years that you live
But by the deeds that you do
     and the joy that you give—
And each day as it comes
     brings a chance to each one
To love to the fullest,
     leaving nothing undone
That would brighten the life
     or lighten the load
Of some weary traveler
     lost on Life's Road—
So what does it matter
     how long we may live
If as long as we live
     we unselfishly give.

Give, and it shall be given unto you;
  good measure, pressed down, and shaken together,
    and running over . . . .

Luke 6:38

The Key

"Unless you become as children"
And love Me as they do,
You cannot enter My Kingdom,
For the door is closed to you . . .
For faith is the key to heaven
And only God's children hold
The key that opens the gateway
To that beautiful City of Gold . . .
For only a child yet unblemished
By the doctrines and theories of man
Is content to Trust and Love Jesus
Without understanding His Plan.

And Jesus called a little child unto him, and set him in the midst of them, And said, Verily I say unto you, Except ye be converted, and become as little children, ye shall not enter into the kingdom of heaven.

Matthew 18:2, 3

Lives Distressed
Cannot Be Blessed

Refuse to be discouraged,
Refuse to be distressed,
For when we are despondent
Our life cannot be blessed—
For doubt and fear and worry
Close the door to *Faith* and *Prayer*,
For there's no room for blessings
When we're lost in deep despair—
So remember when you're troubled
With uncertainty and doubt
It is best to tell *Our Father*
What our fear is all about—
For unless we seek His guidance
When troubled times arise
We are bound to make decisions
That are twisted and unwise—
But when we view our problems
Through the eyes of God above,
Misfortunes turn to blessings
And hatred turns to love.

Fear thou not; for I am with thee:
be not dismayed; for I am thy God:
I will strengthen thee;
yea, I will help thee;
yea, I will uphold thee
with the right hand of my righteousness.
Isaiah 41:10

No Favor Do I Seek Today

I come not to ASK to PLEAD or IMPLORE You,
I just come to tell You HOW MUCH I ADORE YOU,
For to kneel in Your Presence makes me feel blest
For I know that You know all my needs best . . .
And it fills me with joy just to linger with You
As my soul You replenish and my heart You renew,
For prayer is much more than just asking for things—
It's the PEACE and CONTENTMENT that QUIETNESS
brings . . .
So thank You again for Your MERCY and LOVE
And for making me heir to YOUR KINGDOM ABOVE!

Blessed be the Lord,
because he hath heard the voice of my supplications.
The Lord is my strength and my shield;
my heart trusted in him, and I am helped:
therefore my heart greatly rejoiceth;
and with my song will I praise him.

Psalms 28:6, 7

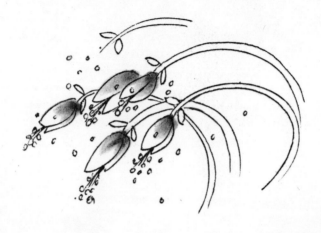

On Life's Busy Thoroughfares We Meet With Angels Unawares

I've never seen God, but I know how I feel . . .
It's people like *you* who make Him *"So Real"* . . .
My God is no stranger, *He's* friendly and gay . . .
And *He* doesn't ask me to weep when I pray . . .
It seems that I pass Him so often each day . . .
In the faces of people I meet on my way . . .
He's the stars in the heaven, a smile on some face . . .
A leaf on a tree or a rose in a vase . . .
He's winter and autumn and summer and spring . . .
In short, *God Is Every Real, Wonderful Thing* . . .
I wish I might meet Him much more than I do . . .
I would if there were *More People Like You.*

Be kindly affectioned one to another with brotherly love; in honour preferring one another; Not slothful in business; fervent in spirit; serving the Lord; Rejoicing in hope; patient in tribulation; continuing instant in prayer; Distributing to the necessity of saints; given to hospitality. Bless them which persecute you: bless, and curse not. Rejoice with them that do rejoice, and weep with them that weep.

Romans 12:10–15

Blessings in Disguise Are Difficult to Recognize

God sends His "little angels"
    in many forms and guises,
They come as lovely miracles
    that God alone devises—
For He does nothing without purpose,
    everything's a perfect plan
To fulfill in bounteous measure
    all He ever promised man—
For every "little angel"
    with a body bent and broken,
Or a little mind retarded
    or little words unspoken,
Is just God's way of trying
    to reach and touch a hand
Of all who do not know Him
    and cannot understand
That often through an angel
    whose "wings will never fly"
The Lord is pointing out the way
    to His eternal sky
Where there will be no handicaps
    of body, soul or mind,
And where all limitations
    will be dropped and left behind—
So accept these "little angels"
    as gifts from God above
And thank Him for this lesson
    in *Faith* and *Hope* and *Love*.

Let brotherly love continue.
Be not forgetful to entertain strangers:
for thereby some have entertained angels unawares.
Hebrews 13:1, 2

51

On the Wings of Prayer

Just close your eyes and open your heart
And feel your worries and cares depart,
Just yield yourself to the Father above
And let Him hold you secure in His love—
For life on earth grows more involved
With endless problems that can't be solved—
But God only asks us to do our best,
Then He will "take over" and finish the rest—
So when you are tired, discouraged and blue,
There's always one door that is open to you—
And that is the door to "The House of Prayer"
And you'll find God waiting to meet you there,
And "The House of Prayer" is no farther away
Than the quiet spot where you kneel and pray—
For the heart is a temple when God is there
As we place ourselves in His loving care,
And He hears every prayer and answers each one
When we pray in His name "THY WILL BE DONE"—
And the burdens that seemed too heavy to bear
Are lifted away on "THE WINGS OF PRAYER."

**The Lord is nigh unto all them that call upon him,
 to all that call upon him in truth.
He will fulfil the desire of them that fear him:
 he also will hear their cry, and will save them.**

Psalms 145:18, 19

God, Give Us "Drive"
But Keep Us From Being "Driven"

There's a difference between "drive" and "driven"—
The one is selfish the other God-given—
For the "driven man" has but one goal,
Just worldly wealth and not "riches of soul,"
And daily he's spurred on to reach and attain
A higher position, more profit and gain,
Ambition and wealth become his great need
As daily he's "driven" by avarice and greed . . .
But most blessed are they who use their "drive"
To work with zeal so all men may survive,
For while they forfeit great personal gain
Their work and their zeal are never in vain . . .
For they contribute to the whole human race
And we cannot survive without growing in grace,
So help us, dear God, to choose between
The "driving force" that rules our routine
So we may make our purpose and goal
Not power and wealth but the growth of our soul . . .
And give us *strength* and *drive* and *desire*
To raise our standards and ethics higher
So all of Us and not *just a few*
May live on earth . . . *as You want Us to.*

For the kingdom of God is not meat and drink; but righteousness, and peace, and joy in the Holy Ghost.

Romans 14:17

A Prayer for the Young and Lovely

Dear God, I keep praying
    For the things I desire,
You tell me I'm selfish
    And "playing with fire"—
It is hard to believe
    I am selfish and vain,
My desires seem so real
    And my needs seem so sane,
And yet You are wiser
    And Your vision is wide
And You look down on me
    And You see deep inside,
You know it's so easy
    To change and distort,
And things that are evil
    Seem so harmless a sport—
Oh, teach me, dear God,
    To not rush ahead
But to pray for Your guidance
    And to trust You instead,
For You know what I need
    And that I'm only a slave
To the things that I want
    And desire and crave—
Oh, God, in your mercy
    Look down on me now
And see in my heart
    That I love You somehow,
Although in my rashness,
    Impatience and greed
I pray for the things
    That I Want and Don't Need—
And instead of a Crown
    Please send me a Cross
And teach me to know
    That All Gain is but Loss,

And show me the way
    To joy without end,
With You as my Father,
    Redeemer and Friend—
And send me the things
    That are hardest to bear,
And keep me forever
    Safe in Thy care.

How shall a young man
steer an honest course?
  By holding to thy word.
           Psalms 119:9 (NEB)

Not to Seek, Lord, but to Share

Dear God, much too often
    we seek You in prayer
Because we are wallowing
    in our own self-despair . . .
We make every word
    we lamentingly speak
An imperative plea
    for whatever we seek . . .
We pray for ourselves
    and so seldom for others,
We're concerned with our problems
    and not with our brothers . . .
We seem to forget, Lord,
    that the "sweet hour of prayer"
Is not for self-seeking
    but to place in Your care
All the lost souls
    unloved and unknown
And to keep praying for them
    until they're YOUR OWN . . .
For it's never enough
    to seek God in prayer
With no thought for others
    who are lost in despair . . .
So teach us, dear God,
    that the POWER of PRAYER
Is made stronger by placing
    THE WORLD IN YOUR CARE!

**Love worketh no ill to his neighbour:
therefore love is the fulfilling of the law.**

Romans 13:10

Keep America in Your Care

We are faced with many problems
        that grow bigger day by day
And, as we seek to solve them
        in our own self-sufficient way,
We keep drifting into chaos
        and our avarice and greed
Blinds us to the answer
        that would help us in our need . .
Oh, God, renew our spirit
        and make us more aware
That our future is dependent
        on sacrifice and prayer,
Forgive us our transgressions
        and revive our faith anew
So we may all draw closer
        to each other and to You . . .
For when a nation is too proud
        to daily kneel and pray
It will crumble into chaos
        and descend into decay,
So stir us with compassion
        and raise our standards higher
And take away our lust for power
        and make our one desire
To be a SHINING SYMBOL
        of ALL THAT'S GREAT AND GOOD
As You lead us in our struggle
        toward NEW-FOUND BROTHERHOOD!

**Blessed is the nation whose God is the Lord; and the people
whom he hath chosen for his own inheritance.**

Psalms 33:12

57

"Seek Ye First
the Kingdom of God"

Life is a mixture
     of sunshine and rain,
Good things and bad things,
     pleasure and pain,
We can't have all sunshine,
     but it's certainly true
There is never a cloud
     the sun doesn't shine through . . .
So always remember
     that whatever betide you
The power of God
     is always beside you,
And if friends disappoint you
     and plans go astray
And nothing works out
     in just the right way,
And you feel you have failed
     in achieving your goal,
And that life wrongly placed you
     in an unfitting role . . .
Take heart and "stand tall"
     and think who you are,
For God is your Father
     and no one can bar
Or keep you from reaching
     your desired success,
Or withhold the joy
     that is yours to possess . . .
For with God on your side
     it matters not who
Is working to keep
     life's good things from you,
For you need nothing more
    than God's guidance and love

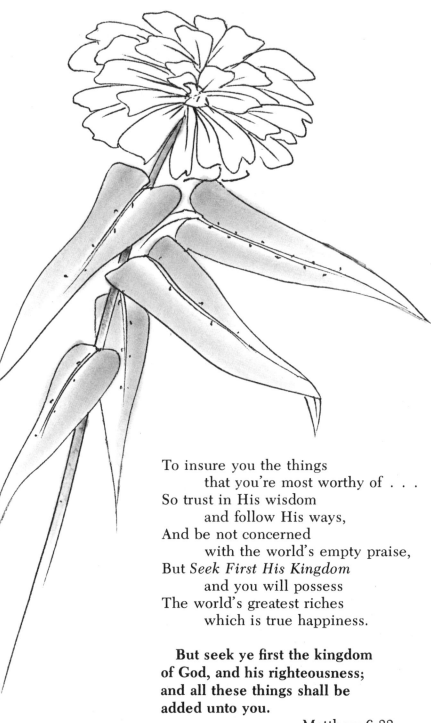

To insure you the things
      that you're most worthy of . . .
So trust in His wisdom
      and follow His ways,
And be not concerned
      with the world's empty praise,
But *Seek First His Kingdom*
      and you will possess
The world's greatest riches
      which is true happiness.

**But seek ye first the kingdom
of God, and his righteousness;
and all these things shall be
added unto you.**

                 Matthew 6:33

Birthdays Are a Gift From God

Where does *time* go in its endless flight—
Spring turns to fall and day to night,
And birthdays come and birthdays go
And where they go we do not know . . .
But God who planned our life on earth
And gave our mind and body birth
And then enclosed a living soul
With heaven as the spirit's goal
Has given man the gift of choice
To follow that small inner voice
That speaks to us from year to year
Reminding us we've naught to fear . . .
For *birthdays* are a *steppingstone*
To endless joys as yet unknown,
So fill each day with happy things
And may your burdens all take wings
And fly away and leave behind
Great joy of heart and peace of mind . . .
For *birthdays* are *the gateway* to
An *endless life of joy for you*
If you but pray from day to day
That He will show you the *Truth* and *The Way.*

**So teach us to number our days, that we may apply our hearts
unto wisdom.**

Psalms 90:12

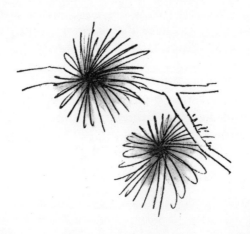

Teach Us to Live

God of love—Forgive! Forgive!
Teach us how to TRULY LIVE,
Ask us not our race or creed,
Just take us in our hour of need,
And let us know You love us, too,
And that we are A PART OF YOU . . .
And someday may man realize
That all the earth, the seas and skies
Belong to God, who made us all,
The rich, the poor, the great, the small,
And in the Father's Holy Sight
No man is yellow, black or white,
And PEACE ON EARTH cannot be found
Until we MEET ON COMMON GROUND
And every man becomes a BROTHER
Who worships God and loves each other.

**Beloved, let us love one another:
for love is of God;
and every one that loveth is born of God,
and knoweth God.**
1 John 4:7

So Swift the Way!
So Short the Day!

In this fast-moving world
     of turmoil and tension,
With problems and troubles,
     too many to mention,
Our days are so crowded
     and our hours are so few,
There's *So Little Time*
     and *So Much To Do* . . .
We are pressured and pushed
     until we are "dizzy",
There's never a minute
     we're not "crazily busy",
And sometimes we wonder
     as we rush through the day—
Does God Really Want Us
     To Hurry This Way?
Why are we impatient
     and continually vexed,

And often bewildered,
      disturbed and perplexed?
Perhaps we're too busy
      with our own selfish seeking
To hear the dear Lord
      when He's tenderly speaking . . .
We are working so tensely
      in our self-centered way,
We've no time for listening
      to what God has to say,
And hard as we work,
      at the end of the day
We know in our hearts
      we did not "pay our way" . . .
But God in His mercy
      looks down on us all,
And though what we've done
      is so pitifully small,
He makes us feel welcome
      to kneel down and pray
For the chance to do better
      as we start a new day,
And life would be better
      if we learned to rely
On our Father in heaven
      without asking *"Why"* . . .
And if we'd remember
      as we rush through the day,
"The Lord Is Our Shepherd
      and *He'll Lead The Way"* . . .
So don't rush ahead
      in reckless endeavor,
Remember *"He Leadeth"*
      and *"Time Is Forever"*!

**. . . let us run with patience
the race that is set before us,
  Looking unto Jesus the author
and finisher of our faith . . . .**
                 Hebrews 12:1, 2

A Teenager's Prayer

God, here I am in a "chaotic state"
Seeking some way to do "something great" . . .
I want to be someone who contributes to make
A less violent world for everyone's sake . . .
But who can I go to and who can I trust,
Who'll show me the difference between love and lust?
I'm willing to listen, I'm willing to do
Whatever it takes to make this world "new" . . .
But in the confusion and the noise all around
Where can the answer to my question be found?
Dear God up in heaven, hear a teen-ager's plea—
Show me somewhere what You want me to be!

This Is All I Ask

Lord, show me the way
I can somehow repay
The blessings *You've* given to me . . .
Lord, teach me to do
What *You* most want me to
And to be what *You* want me to be . . .
I'm unworthy I know
But I do love *You* so—
I beg *You* to answer my plea . . .
I've not got much to give
But as long as I live
May I give it completely to *Thee!*

What Is Life?

Life is a sojourn here on earth
Which begins the day God gives us birth,
We enter this world from the Great Unknown
And God gives each Spirit a form of its own
And endows this form with a heart and a soul
To spur man on to his ultimate goal—
And through the senses of feeling and seeing,
God makes man into a human being
So he may experience a mortal life
And through this period of smiles and strife
Prepare himself to Return as he Came,
For birth and death are in essence the same,
For both are fashioned by God's mighty hand
And, while we cannot understand,
We know we are born to die and arise
For beyond this world in beauty lies
The purpose of living and the ultimate goal
God gives at birth to each seeking soul—
So enjoy your sojourn on earth and be glad
That God gives you a Choice between Good Things and Bad,
And only be sure that you Heed God's Voice
Whenever life asks you to make a choice.

Oh that men would praise the Lord for his goodness, and for his wonderful works to the children of men!

For he satisfieth the longing soul, and filleth the hungry soul with goodness.

Psalms 107:8, 9

A Tribute to All Daughters

Every home should have a daughter,
    for there's nothing like a girl
To keep the world around her
    in one continuous whirl . . .
From the moment she arrives on earth,
    and on through womanhood,
A daughter is a *female*
    who is seldom understood . . .
One minute she is laughing,
    the next she starts to cry,
Man just can't understand her
    and there's just no use to try . . .
She is soft and sweet and cuddly,
    but she's also wise and smart,
She's a wondrous combination
    of a mind and brain and heart . . .
And even in her baby days
    she's just a born coquette,
And anything she really wants
    she manages to get . . .
For even at a tender age
    she uses all her wiles
And she can melt the hardest heart
    with the sunshine of her smiles . . .
She starts out as a rosebud
    with her beauty unrevealed
Then through a happy childhood
    her petals are unsealed . . .
She's soon a sweet girl graduate,
    and then a blushing bride,
And then a lovely woman
    as the rosebud opens wide . . .
And some day in the future,
    if it be God's precious will,

She, too, will be a Mother
　　　and know that reverent thrill
That comes to every Mother
　　　whose heart is filled with love
When she beholds the "angel"
　　　that God sent her from above . . .
And there would be no life at all
　　　in this world or the other
Without a *darling daughter*
　　　who, in turn, becomes a *mother!*

What Does God Know of These Modern Days?

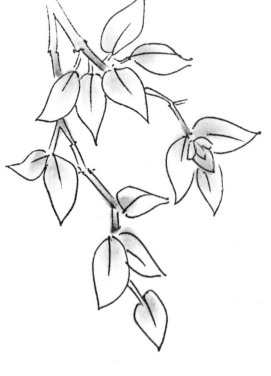

He sent His son to live on earth
And to walk with sinful men,
And the problems that confront us
Are the same Today as Then,
For vice and crime and evil
Prevailed in Rome and Greece
And power-driven demagogues
Incited war, not peace—
There was violence and dissension
And injustice in high courts,
And slayings were accepted
As one of the favorite sports—
Depraved, debauched and dissolute,
Men lusted after pleasure,
They knew no god but Power
And Gold was their only treasure—
So all the things we face today
Are certainly not new
And the Son of God experienced
Everything We're Going Through—
So let no one mislead you
With that hackneyed little phrase
That there's a "many-century gap"
Between God and Modern Days—
For God has seen a lot of worlds
In this same tragic state
And He knows that we are headed for
The same, grim, terrible fate
Unless man is awakened
Before the hour's too late
And at long last realizes
That God's Always Up-To-Date!

It is not that the Lord is slow in fulfilling his promise, as some
suppose, but that he is very patient with you, because it is not
his will for any to be lost, but for all to come to repentance.
2 Peter 3:9 (NEB)

Death Opens the Door
to Life Evermore

We live a short while on earth below,
Reluctant to die for we do not know
Just what "dark death" is all about
And so we view it with fear and doubt,
Not certain of what is around the bend
We look on death as the final end
To all that made us a mortal being
And yet there lies just beyond our seeing
A beautiful life so full and complete
That we should leave with hurrying feet
To walk with God by sacred streams
Amid beauty and peace beyond our dreams—
For all who believe in the RISEN LORD
Have been assured of this reward,
And death for them is just "graduation"
To a higher realm of wide elevation—
For life on earth is a transient affair,
Just a few brief years in which to prepare
For a life that is free from pain and tears
Where time is not counted by hours or years—
For death is only the method God chose
To colonize heaven with the souls of those
Who by their apprenticeship on earth
Proved worthy to dwell in the land of new birth—
So death is not sad . . . it's a time for elation,
A joyous transition . . . the soul's emigration
Into a place where the soul's SAFE and FREE
To live with God through ETERNITY!

**For I am persuaded, that neither death, nor life, nor angels,
nor principalities, nor powers, nor things present, nor things to
come, Nor height, nor depth, nor any other creature, shall be
able to separate us from the love of God, which is in Christ
Jesus our Lord.**

Romans 8:38, 39

The Meaning of True Love

It is sharing and caring,
Giving and forgiving,
Loving and being loved,
Walking hand in hand,
Talking heart to heart,
Seeing through each other's eyes,
Laughing together,
Weeping together,
Praying together,
And always trusting
And believing
And thanking GOD
For each other . . .
For love that is shared
        is a beautiful thing—
It enriches the soul
        and makes the heart sing!

What Will You Do
With This Year That's So New?

As we start a new year
untouched and unmarred,
Unblemished and flawless,
unscratched and unscarred,
May we try to do better and accomplish much more
And be kinder and wiser
than in the year gone before—
Let us wipe our slates clean
and start over again,
For God gives this privilege to all sincere men
Who will humbly admit they have failed many ways
But are willing to try and improve these "new days"
By asking God's help in all that they do
And counting on Him to refresh and renew
Their courage and faith when things go wrong
And the way seems dark
and the road rough and long—
What Will You Do
With This Year That's So New???
The choice is yours—God leaves that to *You!*

. . . **choose you this day whom ye will serve** . . . .
Joshua 24:15

Time Is a Gift of God

We stand once more
on the threshold
of a shining and unblemished year,
Untouched yet by *Time* and *Frustration*,
unclouded by *Failure* and *Fear* . . .
How will we use the days of this year
and the *Time* God has placed in our hands,
Will we waste the minutes
and squander the hours,
leaving "no prints behind in time's sands" . . .
Will we vainly complain
that *Life* is *So Swift*,
that we haven't the *Time to Do Good,*
Our days are too crowded,
our hours are too short
to do *All the Good Things* we should . . .
We say we would pray
if we just had the time,
and be kind to all those in need,
But we live in a world
of *"Planned Progress"*
and our national password is *"Speed"* . . .
God, grant us the grace
as another year starts
to use all the hours of our days,
Not for our own selfish interests
and our own willful, often-wrong ways . . .
But teach us
to *Take Time for Praying*
and to find time
for *Listening to You*
So each day is spent
well and wisely
doing *What You Most Want Us to Do.*

A Prayer for the New Year

God grant us this year a wider view
So we see others' faults through the eyes of YOU—
Teach us to judge not with hasty tongue,
Neither THE ADULT . . . or THE YOUNG,
Give us patience and grace to endure
And a stronger faith so we feel secure,
And instead of remembering, help us to forget
The irritations that caused us to fret,
Freely forgiving for some offence
And finding each day a rich recompense
In offering a friendly, helping hand
And trying in all ways to understand
That ALL OF US whoever we are
Are trying to reach "an unreachable star"—
For the GREAT and SMALL . . . the GOOD and BAD,
The YOUNG and OLD . . . the SAD and GLAD
Are asking today, "IS LIFE WORTH LIVING?"
And the ANSWER is only in LOVING and GIVING—
For only LOVE can make man kind
And KINDNESS of HEART brings PEACE of MIND,
And by giving love we can start this year
To lift the clouds of HATE and FEAR.

**And be ye kind one to another,
tenderhearted, forgiving one another,
even as God for Christ's sake hath forgiven you.**
Ephesians 4:32

76

Make the New Year
a Stepping-Stone
to Growth

Whatever the new year has in store
Remember there's always a good reason for
Everything that comes into our life,
For even in times of struggle and strife
If we but lift our eyes above
We see "our cross" as a "gift of love" . . .
For things that cause the heart to ache
Until we feel that it must break
Become the strength by which we climb
To higher heights that are sublime . . .
So welcome every stumbling block
And every thorn and jagged rock,
For each one is a *Stepping-Stone*
To a fuller life than we've ever known,
And in the radiance of God's smiles
We learn to soar above life's trials . . .
So let us accept what the new year brings,
Seeing the *Hand of God* in *All Things*,
And as we grow in strength and grace
The clearer we can see God's face.

Beloved, now are we the sons of God, and it doth not yet appear what we shall be: but we know that, when he shall appear, we shall be like him; for we shall see him as he is.

1 John 3:2

A New Year Meditation

What better time
and what better season,
What greater occasion
or more wonderful reason
To kneel down in prayer and lift
our hands high
To the God of creation who made
earth and sky,
Who sent us His Son
to live here among men
And the message He brought
is as true *Now* as *Then*—
So at this glad season
when there's joy everywhere
Let us meet our Redeemer
at *The Altar of Prayer*
Asking Him humbly to bless all of our days
And grant us forgiveness for our erring ways—
And though we're unworthy,
dear Father above,

Accept us today and let us dwell
in Thy Love
So we may grow stronger,
upheld by Thy grace,
And with Thy assistance
be able to face
All the temptations
that fill every day,
And hold onto our hands
when we stumble and stray—
And thank you, dear God,
for the year that now ends
And for the great blessing
of loved ones and friends.

**For we have not an high priest which cannot be touched with
the feeling of our infirmities; but was in all points tempted like
as we are, yet without sin. Let us therefore come boldly unto the
throne of grace, that we may obtain mercy, and find grace to
help in time of need.**

Hebrews 4:15, 16

A New Year Brings
a New Beginning

As the New Year starts
and the old year ends
There's no better time to make amends
For all the things we sincerely regret
And wish in our hearts
we could somehow forget—
We all make mistakes,
for it's human to err,
But no one need ever give up in despair,
For God gives us all
a brand-new beginning,
A chance to start over
and repent of our sinning—
And when God forgives us we too must forgive
And resolve to do better
each day that we live
By constantly trying
to be like Him more nearly
And to trust in His wisdom
and love Him more dearly—
Assured that we're never out of His care
And we're always welcome to seek Him in prayer.

**Come unto me, all ye that labour
and are heavy laden, and I will give you rest.**
Matthew 11:28

A New Year! A New Day! A New Life!

Not only on *New Year's* but all the year through
God gives us a chance to begin life anew,
For each day at dawning we have but to pray
That all the mistakes that we made yesterday
Will be blotted out and forgiven by grace,
For God in His love will completely efface
All that is past and He'll grant a new start
To all who are truly repentant at heart—
And well may man pause in awesome-like wonder
That Our Father in heaven who dwells far asunder
Could still remain willing to freely forgive
The shabby, small lives we so selfishly live
And still would be mindful of sin-ridden man
Who constantly goes on defying God's Plan—
But this is the *Gift* of God's limitless love
A gift that we all are so unworthy of,
But God gave it to us and all we need do
Is to ask God's forgiveness and begin life anew.

Faith Is a Mighty Fortress

We stand once more at the end of the year
With mixed emotions of *hope* and *fear*,
Hope for *the Peace* we long have sought,
Fear that *our hopes* will come to naught . . .
Unwilling to trust in the *Father's Will*,
We count on our logic and shallow skill
And, in our arrogance and pride,
Man is no longer satisfied
To place his confidence and love
With *Childlike Faith* in God above . . .
But tiny hands and tousled heads
That kneel in prayer by little beds
Are closer to the dear Lord's heart
And of His Kingdom more a part
Than we who search and never find
The answers to our questioning mind,
For faith in things we cannot see
Requires a child's simplicity . . .
Oh, Father, grant once more to men
A simple *Childlike Faith* again,
Forgetting *color, race* and *creed*
And seeing only the heart's deep need . . .
For Faith alone can save man's soul
And lead him to a *higher goal*,
For there's but one unfailing course—
We win by *Faith* and *not* by *Force*.

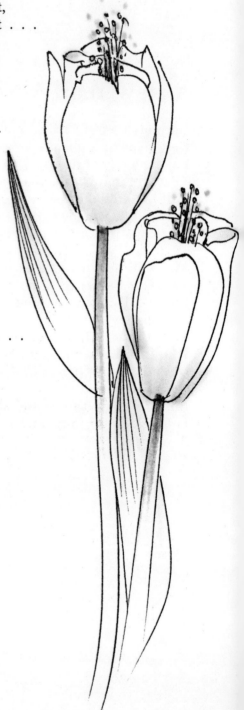

God, Grant Us Hope
and Faith and Love

HOPE for a world
      grown cynically cold,
Hungry for power
      and greedy for gold . . .

FAITH to believe
      when within and without
There's nameless fear
      in a world of doubt . . .

LOVE that is bigger
      than race or creed,
To cover the world
      and fulfil each need . . .

God, grant these gifts
      To all troubled hearts
As the old year ends
      And a new year starts.

So faith, hope, love abide, these three;
but the greatest of these is love.
                    1 Corinthians 13:13 (RSV)

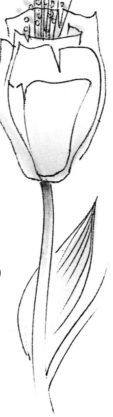

Ireland Is the Land of Love, Legends and Laughter

There are many, many legends
about St. Patrick's Day,
About the *Shamrock*
and the *Blarney*
and the *Leprechauns* at play,
And that most delightful story
that God blessed
the *Emerald Isle*
With the *Beauty of His Goodness*
and the *Sunshine of His Smile*,
And how a dear,
beloved *Saint*
taught the *Irish* about *God*
Just by showing them
a *Shamrock*
that was grown on Erin's sod . . .
He told them of the *Trinity*,
the *Living Three* in *One*,
The *Holy Ghost* . . . the *Father*,
and *His Beloved Son* . . .

And all these lovely legends
of the well-loved Irish race
Have given every Irishman
A *Very Special Place*
Not only just in history
but in everybody's heart,
For of this old earth's laughter,
the dearest, finest part
Is made of "smiling Irish eyes"
and mirth-filled Irish jokes—
And what a dull world
this would be
without *God's Irish Folks*.

A merry heart doeth good like a medicine . . . .
Proverbs 17:22

"After the Winter . . .
God Sends the Spring"

Easter is a season
Of HOPE and JOY and CHEER,
There's beauty all around us
To see and touch and hear . . .
So, no matter how downhearted
And discouraged we may be,
New Hope is born when we behold
Leaves budding on a tree . . .
Or when we see a timid flower
Push through the frozen sod
And open wide in glad surprise
Its petaled eyes to God . . .
For this is just God saying—
"Lift up your eyes to Me,
And the bleakness of your spirit,
Like the budding springtime tree,
Will lose its wintery darkness
And your heavy heart will sing"—
For GOD never sends THE WINTER
Without THE JOY OF SPRING.

My times are in thy hand . . . .
                    Psalms 31:15

86

Easter Is a Time
of Many Miracles

Flowers sleeping 'neath the snow,
Awakening when the Spring winds blow;
Leafless trees so bare before,
Gowned in lacy green once more;
Hard, unyielding, frozen sod
Now softly carpeted by God;
Still streams melting in the Spring,
Rippling over rocks that sing;
Barren, windswept, lonely hills
Turning gold with daffodils . . .
These miracles are all around
Within our sight and touch and sound,
As true and wonderful today
As when "the stone was rolled away"
Proclaiming to all doubting men
That in God all things live again.

An Easter Meditation

In the glorious Easter Story
A troubled world can find
Blessed reassurance
And enduring peace of mind—
For though we grow discouraged
In this world we're living in,
There is comfort just in knowing
That God triumphed over sin,
For our Saviour's Resurrection
Was God's way of telling men
That in Christ we are eternal
And in Him we live again—
And to know life is unending
And God's love is endless, too,
Makes our daily tasks and burdens
So much easier to do,
And our earthly trials and problems
Are but guideposts on the way
To the love and life eternal
That God promised Easter Day.

. . . [Jesus Christ] hath abolished death, and hath brought life and immortality to light through the gospel.

2 Timothy 1:10

Springtime Glory

Flowers buried
beneath the snow
Awakening again to live and grow—
Leaves that fell to the earth to die
Enriching the soil in which they lie—
Lifeless-looking, stark,
stripped trees
Bursting with buds
in the Springtime breeze
Are just a few examples of
The greatness of God's power and love,
And in this blaze of Springtime glory
Just who could doubt
the Easter Story!

An Easter Prayer

God, give us eyes to see
      the beauty of the Spring,
And to behold Your majesty
      in every living thing—
And may we see in lacy leaves
      and every budding flower
The Hand that rules the universe
      with gentleness and power—
And may this Easter grandeur
      that Spring lavishly imparts
Awaken faded flowers of faith
      lying dormant in our hearts,
And give us ears to hear, dear God,
      the Springtime song of birds
With messages more meaningful
      than man's often empty words
Telling harried human beings
      who are lost in dark despair—
"Be like us and do not worry
      for God has you in His care."

**Look at the birds of the air; they
do not sow and reap and store
in barns, yet your heavenly Father
feeds them. You are worth
more than the birds!**
                Matthew 6:26 (NEB)

An Easter Prayer for Peace

Our Father, up in heaven,
    hear this Easter prayer:
May the people of ALL NATIONS
    BE UNITED IN THY CARE,
For earth's peace and man's salvation
    can come only by Thy grace
And not through bombs and missiles
    and our quest for outer space . . .
For until all men recognize
    that "THE BATTLE IS THE LORD'S"
And peace on earth can not be won
    with strategy and swords,
We will go on vainly fighting,
    as we have in ages past,
Finding only empty victories
    and a peace that cannot last . . .
But we've grown so rich and mighty
    and so arrogantly strong,
We no longer ask in humbleness—
    "God, show us where we're wrong" . . .
We have come to trust completely
    in the power of man-made things,
Unmindful of God's mighty power
    and that HE IS "KING OF KINGS" . . .
We have turned our eyes from HIM
    to go our selfish way,
And money, power, and pleasure
    are the gods we serve today . . .

And the good green earth God gave us
      to peacefully enjoy,
Through greed and fear and hatred
      we are seeking to destroy . . .
Oh, Father, up in heaven,
      stir and wake our sleeping souls,
Renew our faith and lift us up
      and give us higher goals,
And grant us heavenly guidance
      as Easter comes again—
For, more than GUIDED MISSILES,
      all the world needs GUIDED MEN.

The Lord is good,
  a strong hold in the day of trouble;
    and he knoweth them that trust in him.
Nahum 1:7

An Easter Promise

If we but had the eyes to see
God's face in every cloud,
If we but had the ears to hear
His voice above the crowd
If we could feel His gentle touch
In every Springtime breeze
And find a haven in His arms
'Neath sheltering, leafy trees . . .
If we could just lift up our hearts
Like flowers to the sun
And trust His *Easter Promise*
And pray, *"Thy Will Be Done"*,
We'd find the peace we're seeking,
The kind no man can give,
The peace that comes from knowing
He Died So We Might Live!

For God so loved the world, that he gave his only begotten Son, that whosoever believeth in him should not perish, but have everlasting life.

John 3:16

Easter Reflections

With OUR EYES we see
the beauty of Easter
as the earth awakens once more . . .

With OUR EARS we hear
the birds sing sweetly
to tell us Spring again is here . . .

With OUR HANDS we pick
the golden daffodils
and the fragrant hyacinths . . .

But only with OUR HEARTS
can we feel the MIRACLE of GOD'S LOVE
which redeems all men . . .

And only with OUR SOUL
can we make our "pilgrimage to God"
and inherit His Easter Gift of ETERNAL LIFE.

Eternal Spring

Easter comes with cheeks a-glowing,
      flowers bloom and streams are flowing,
And the earth in glad surprise
      opens wide its Springtime eyes . . .
All nature heeds the call of Spring
      as God awakens everything,
And all that seemed so dead and still
      experiences a sudden thrill
As Springtime lays a magic hand
      across God's vast and fertile land . . .
Oh, how can anyone stand by
      and watch a sapphire, Springtime sky,
Or see a fragile flower break through
      what just a day ago or two
Seemed barren ground still hard with frost,
      but in God's world no life is lost . . .
And flowers sleep beneath the ground
      but when they hear Spring's waking sound
They push themselves through layers of clay
      to reach the sunlight of God's Day . . .
And man, like flowers, too, must sleep
      until he is called from the "darkened deep" . . .
To live in that place where angels sing
      And where there is Eternal Spring!

For our light affliction, which is but for a moment, worketh for us a far more exceeding and eternal weight of glory; while we look not at the things which are seen, but at the things which are not seen: for the things which are seen are temporal; but the things which are not seen are eternal.

2 Corinthians 4:17, 18

The Hope of the World

An *Empty Tomb* . . .
    a *Stone Rolled Away*
Speak of the Saviour
    who rose Easter Day . . .
But that was centuries
    and centuries ago,
And we ask today
    Was It Really So?
Did He walk on earth
    and live and die
And return to *His Father*
    To Dwell on High?
We were not there
    to hear or see,
But our hopes and dreams
    of *Eternity*
Are centered around
    The Easter Story
When Christ ascended
    and rose in glory . . .
And life on earth
    has not been the same,
Regardless of what
    the skeptics claim . . .
For, after the Lord
    was crucified,
Even the ones who had
    scoffed and denied
Knew that something
    had taken place
That nothing could ever
    remove or erase . . .
For *Hope* was born
    in the soul of man,
And *Faith* to believe
    in God's *Master Plan*

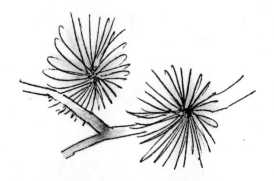

Stirred in the hearts
    to dispel doubt and fear
And that Faith has grown
    with each passing year . . .
For the *Hope* of *Man*
    is *The Easter Story,*
For life is robbed
    of all meaning and glory
Unless man knows
    that he has a "goal"
And a "resting place"
    for his searching soul.

Behold, I shew you a mystery; We shall not all sleep, but we shall all be changed, In a moment, in the twinkling of an eye, at the last trump: for the trumpet shall sound, and the dead shall be raised incorruptible, and we shall be changed. For this corruptible must put on incorruption, and this mortal must put on immortality. So when this corruptible shall have put on incorruption, and this mortal shall have put on immortality, then shall be brought to pass the saying that is written, Death is swallowed up in victory. O death, where is thy sting? O grave, where is thy victory? The sting of death is sin; and the strength of sin is the law. But thanks be to God, which giveth us the victory through our Lord Jesus Christ. Therefore, my beloved brethren, be ye steadfast, unmoveable, always abounding in the work of the Lord, forasmuch as ye know that your labour is not in vain in the Lord.

1 Corinthians 15:51–58

Let Us Pray at This Glorious Easter Season

What better time
    or more beautiful season,
What greater occasion
    or more wonderful reason
To kneel down in prayer
    and thank God above
For Eternal Life
    the Gift of His Love—
For in sending His Son
    to be crucified
He granted man Life
    because His Son died—
So at this glad season
    when there's joy everywhere
Let us meet Our Redeemer
    at The Altar of Prayer.

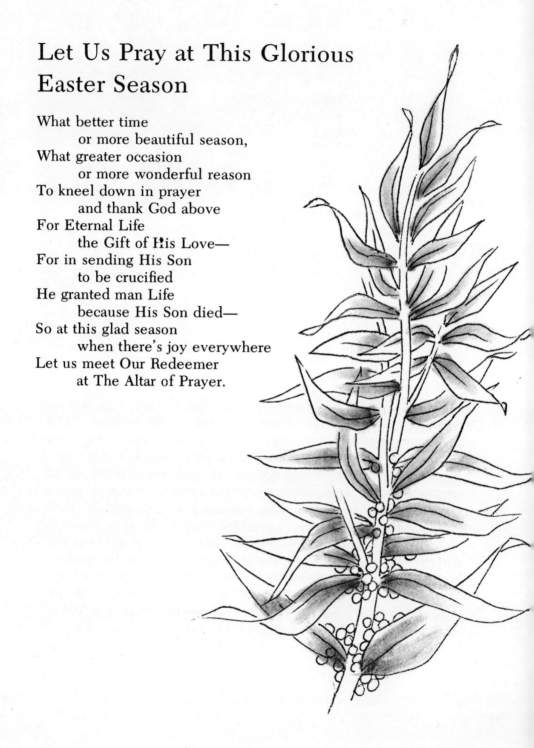

What Is Christmas?

Is it just a day
        at the end of the year?
A gay holiday filled
        with merry good cheer?
A season for presents—
        both taking and giving?
A time to indulge
        in the pleasures of living?
Are we lost in a meaningless,
        much-muddled daze
That covers our minds
        like a grey autumn haze?
Have we closed our eyes
        to God and His love?
And turned our eyes
        from "THE BRIGHT STAR ABOVE?"
Oh, Father in heaven,
        renew and restore
The real, true meaning
        of Christmas once more,
So we can feel
        in our hearts again
That "PEACE ON EARTH,
        GOOD WILL TO MEN"
Is still a promise
        that man can claim
If "HE BUT SEEKS IT
        IN THY NAME."

And there were in the same country shepherds abiding in the field, keeping watch over their flock by night. And, lo, the angel of the Lord came upon them, and the glory of the Lord shone round about them: and they were sore afraid.

And the angel said unto them, Fear not: for, behold, I bring you good tidings of great joy, which shall be to all people. For unto you is born this day in the city of David a Saviour, which is Christ the Lord. And this shall be a sign unto you; Ye shall find the babe wrapped in swaddling clothes, lying in a manger. And suddenly there was with the angel a multitude of the heavenly host praising God, and saying, Glory to God in the highest, and on earth peace, good will toward men.

Luke 2:8–14

We've Come a Long Way Since That First Christmas Day

We've come a long way
     since that first Christmas Night
When led by a STAR
     so wondrously bright
The Wise Men journeyed
     to find the place
That cradled the CHRIST CHILD'S
     beautiful face—
But like "lost sheep"
     we have wandered away
From God and His Son
     who was born Christmas Day,
And instead of depending
     on God's guiding hand
Ingenious man has assumed
     full command
Like the "Prodigal Son"
     who seeks to be free
From the heavenly FATHER
     and His holy decree—
But life without God
     is corroding man's soul,
Weakening his spirit
     and distorting his goal,
And unless we return
     to OUR FATHER again
We will never have PEACE
     and GOOD WILL among men—
And the freedom man sought
     will make him a slave
For only through God
     is man strong, free and brave,
So let us return
     to OUR FATHER and pray
That CHRIST is reborn
     in our hearts Christmas Day.

Was It Really So?

A Star in the sky, an Angel's voice
Telling the world—REJOICE! REJOICE!
But that was centuries and centuries ago,
And we ask today, WAS IT REALLY SO?
Was the Christ Child born in a manger bed
Without a pillow to rest His head?
Did He walk on earth and live and die
And return to God to dwell on high?

We were not there to hear or see,
But our hopes and dreams of ETERNITY
Are centered around that holy story
When God sent us HIS SON IN GLORY—
And life on earth has not been the same,
Regardless of what the skeptics claim,
For no event ever left behind
A transformation of this kind . . .

So question and search and doubt, if you will,
But the STORY OF CHRISTMAS is living still . . .
And though man may conquer the earth and the sea,
He cannot conquer ETERNITY . . .
And with all his triumph man is but a clod
UNTIL HE COMES TO REST WITH GOD.

Let Us Live Christmas Every Day

Christmas is more than a day
    at the end of the year,
More than a season
    of joy and good cheer,
Christmas is really
    God's pattern for living
To be followed all year
    by unselfish giving . . .
For the holiday season
    awakens good cheer
And draws us closer
    to those we hold dear,
And we open our hearts
    and find it is Good
To live among men
    as WE ALWAYS SHOULD . . .
But as soon as the tinsel
    is stripped from the tree
The spirit of Christmas
    fades silently
Into the background
    of daily routine
And is lost in the whirl
    of life's busy scene,
And all unawares
    we miss and forego
The greatest blessing
    that mankind can know . . .

For if we lived Christmas
      each day, as we should,
And made it our aim
      to always do good,
We'd find the lost key
      to meaningful living
That comes not from GETTING,
      but from unselfish GIVING . . .
And we'd know the great joy
      of PEACE UPON EARTH
Which was the real purpose
      of our Saviour's birth,
For in the GLAD TIDINGS
      of the first Christmas Night,
God showed us THE WAY
      AND THE TRUTH AND THE LIGHT!

But the fruit of the Spirit is love, joy, peace, longsuffering, gentleness, goodness, faith, Meekness, temperance: against such there is no law.

Galatians 5:22, 23

107

The Priceless
Gift of Christmas

Now Christmas is a season
    for joy and merrymaking,
A time for gifts and presents,
    for giving and for taking . . .
A festive, friendly, happy time
    when everyone is gay—
But have we ever really felt
    the GREATNESS of the Day? . . .
For through the centuries the world
    has wandered far away
From the beauty and the meaning
    of the HOLY CHRISTMAS DAY . .
For Christmas is a heavenly gift
    that only God can give,
It's ours just for the asking,
    for as long as we shall live,
It can't be bought or bartered,
    it can't be won or sold,
It doesn't cost a penny
    and it's worth far more than gold . .
It isn't bright and gleaming
    for eager eyes to see,
It can't be wrapped in tinsel
    or placed beneath a tree . . .
It isn't soft and shimmering
    for reaching hands to touch,
Or some expensive luxury
    you've wanted very much . . .

For the PRICELESS GIFT OF CHRISTMAS
     is meant just for the heart
And we receive it only
     when we become a part
Of the kingdom and the glory
     which is ours to freely take,
For God sent the Holy Christ Child
     at Christmas for our sake,
So man might come to know Him
     and feel His Presence near
And see the many miracles
     performed while He was here . . .
And this PRICELESS GIFT OF CHRISTMAS
     is within the reach of all,
The rich, the poor, the young and old,
     the greatest and the small . . .
So take HIS PRICELESS GIFT OF LOVE,
     REACH OUT and YOU RECEIVE,
And the only payment that God asks
     is just that YOU BELIEVE.

"The Miracle of Christmas"

The wonderment
    in a small child's eyes,
The ageless awe
    in the Christmas skies,
The nameless joy
    that fills the air,
The throngs that kneel
    in praise and prayer . . .
These are the things
    that make us know
That men may come
    and men may go,
But none will
    ever find a way
To banish Christ
    from Christmas Day . . .
For with each child
    there's born again
A *Mystery* that baffles men.

If There Had Never Been a Christmas

If God had never sent His Son
    To dwell with man on earth,
If there had been no Christmas
    To herald the Christ Child's birth,
If in this world of violence
    And hatred, crime and war
There were absolutely nothing
    That made life worth living for,
If whenever man was troubled
    And lost in loneliness
There were no haven for his heart
    To calm his restlessness,
Then life would be intolerable
    And loathsome with disgust,
For there would be no love at all,
    Just ugliness and lust—
And there would be no Easter
    And no resurrected Lord,
No promise of Eternity
    And no heavenly reward—
So let us thank Our Father
    That He sent His Only Son
So after this life's ended
    And our work on earth is done
There's the promise of Eternity
    Where our "cross" becomes a "crown"
When all our trials are over
    And we lay our burden down.

"God So Loved the World"

Our Father up in Heaven,
    long, long years ago,
Looked down in His great mercy
    upon the earth below
And saw that folk were lonely
    and lost in deep despair
And so He said, "I'll send My Son
    to walk among them there . . .
So they can hear Him speaking
    and feel His nearness, too,
And see the many miracles
    that Faith alone can do . . .
For if man really sees Him
    and can touch His healing hand
I know it will be easier
    to Believe and Understand" . . .
And so The Holy Christ Child
    came down to live on earth
And that is why we celebrate
    His holy, wondrous birth,
And that is why at Christmas
    the world becomes aware
That heaven may seem far away
    but God is Everywhere.

"Glory to God in the Highest"

"Glory to God in the highest
And peace on earth to men"—
May the Christmas song the angels sang
Stir in our hearts again
And bring a new awareness
That the fate of every nation
Is sealed securely in the hand
Of the *Maker of Creation* . . .
For man, with all his knowledge,
His inventions and his skill,
Can never go an inch beyond
The holy Father's will . . .
For all of man's achievements
Are so puny and so small,
Just "ant hills" in the kingdom
Of the God who made us all . . .
For, greater than the scope of man
And far beyond all seeing,
In Him who made the universe,
Man lives and has his being . . .
For it took an all-wise Father
To hang the stars in space,
And keep the earth and sky and sea
Securely in their place . . .
And man can never penetrate
The Father's *Master Plan*—
For only God in heaven
Can control the fate of man.

"The Fruit of the Spirit Is Love and Peace"

There is no thinking person
Who can stand untouched today
And view the world around us
Slowly drifting to decay
Without feeling deep within him
A silent, unnamed dread
As he contemplates the future
That lies frighteningly ahead . . .
For, like watching storm clouds gather
In a dark and threatening sky,
Man knows that there is nothing
He can formulate or try
That will stop the storm from breaking
In its fury and its force,
Nor can he change or alter
The storm's destructive course,
But his anxious fears are lessened
When he calls on God above,
For he knows above the storm clouds
Is the brightness of God's love . . .

So as the *"clouds of chaos"*
Gather in man's muddled mind,
And he searches for the answer
He *alone* can never find,
Let us recognize we're facing
Problems man has never solved,
And with all our daily efforts
Life grows more and more involved,
But our future will seem brighter
And we'll meet with less resistance
If we call upon our Father
And seek Divine Assistance . . .
For the spirit can unravel
Many tangled, knotted threads
That defy the skill and power
Of the world's best hands and heads,
And our plans for growth and progress,
Of which we all have dreamed,
Cannot survive materially
Unless *our spirits* are redeemed . . .
So may our prayer this Christmas
Be that God may dwell again
In human hearts throughout the world
And bring *Good Will* to men.

"The Gift of God's Love"

All over the world at this season,
Expectant hands reach to receive
Gifts that are lavishly fashioned,
The finest that man can conceive . . .
For, purchased and given at Christmas
Are luxuries we long to possess,
Given as favors and tokens
To try in some way to express
That strange, indefinable feeling
Which is part of this glad time of year
When streets are crowded with shoppers
And the air resounds with good cheer . . .
But back of each tinsel-tied package
Exchanged at this gift-giving season,
Unrecognized often by many,
Lies a deeper, more meaningful reason . . .
For, born in a manger at Christmas
As a gift from the Father above,
An infant whose name was called Jesus
Brought mankind the GIFT OF GOD'S LOVE . . .
And the gifts that we give have no purpose
Unless God is a part of the giving,
And unless we make Christmas a pattern
To be followed in everyday living.

Each Christmas
God Renews His Promise

Long, long ago in a land far away,
There came the dawn
    of The First Christmas Day,
And each year we see that promise reborn
That God gave the world
    on that first Christmas Morn . . .
For the silent stars in the timeless skies
And the wonderment
    in a small child's eyes.
The Christmas songs the carollers sing,
The tidings of joy
    that the Christmas bells ring
Remind us again of that Still, Silent Night
When the heavens shone
    with a wondrous Light,
And the angels sang of Peace on Earth
And told men of
The Christ Child's Birth—
For Christmas is more than a Beautiful Story,
It's the promise of life
    and Eternal Glory.

A Christmas Prayer

"O GOD, OUR HELP IN AGES PAST,
     OUR HOPE IN YEARS TO BE"—
Look down upon this PRESENT
     And see our need of Thee . . .
For in this age of unrest,
     With danger all around,
We need Thy hand to lead us
     To higher, safer ground . . .
We need Thy help and counsel
     To make us more aware
That our safety and security
     Lie solely in Thy care . . .
And so we pray this Christmas
     To feel THY PRESENCE near
And for Thy all-wise guidance
     Throughout the coming year . . .
First, give us understanding
     Enough to make us kind,
So we may judge all people
     With our heart and not our mind,
Then give us strength and courage
     To be honorable and true
And place our trust implicitly
     In "UNSEEN THINGS" and "YOU" . . .
And help us when we falter
     And renew our faith each day
And forgive our human errors
     And hear us when we pray,
And keep us gently humble
     In the GREATNESS OF THY LOVE
So some day we are fit to dwell
     With Thee in *Peace Above*.

Christmas and
the Christ Child

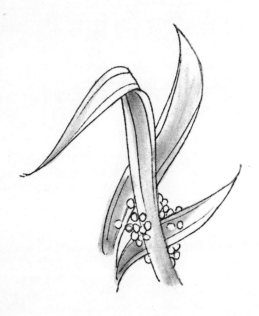

In our Christmas celebrations
Of merriment and mirth
Let's not forget the *Miracle*
    Of the
Holy Christ Child's Birth—
For in our gay festivities
It is easy to lose sight
    Of the
Baby in the Manger
And that *Holy Silent Night* . . .

And we miss the mighty meaning
And we lose the greater glory
    Of the
Holy Little Christ Child
And the blessed *Christmas Story*
    If we don't
Keep Christ in Christmas
And make *His Love* a part
Of all the joy and happiness
That fill our home
    and heart.

**Jesus Christ the same yesterday,
and to day, and for ever.**
Hebrews 13:8

"The Blessed Assurance of Christmas"

In the wondrous Christmas Story
    a troubled world can find
Blessed reassurance
    and enduring peace of mind—
For though we grow discouraged
    in the world we're living in,
There is a comfort just in knowing
    that God triumphed over sin
By sending us His Only Son
    to live among us here
So He might know and understand
    man's loneliness and fear—
And for our soul's salvation
    Christ was born and lived and died,
For life became immortal
    when God's Son was crucified,
And the Christ Child's *Resurrection*
    was God's way of telling men
That in Christ we are Eternal
    and in Him we live again—
And to know that life is endless
    puts new purpose in our days
And fills our hearts with joyous songs
    of hope and love and praise . . .
For to know that through the Christ Child
    our spirits were redeemed
And that God has stored up treasures
    beyond all that man has dreamed
Is a promise that is priceless
    and it's ours if we but say

That "in so far as in us lies"
    we will follow in His ways—
For God our Heavenly Father
    and Christ, His Only Son
Will forgive us our transgressions
    and the misdeeds we have done
If we but yield our hearts to God
    and ask but one reward—
"The joy of walking daily
    in the *Footsteps of The Lord.*"

"Behold, I Bring You
Good Tidings of Great Joy"

"Glad Tidings" herald
 the Christ Child's birth—
"Joy To The World" and "Peace On Earth"—
"Glory To God"—let all men rejoice
And harken once more
 to the "Angel's Voice" . . .

It matters not Who or What you are,
All men can behold "The Christmas Star"—
For the Star that shone is shining still
In the hearts of men
 of Peace and Good Will,
It offers the answer
 to every man's need,
Regardless of color or race or creed . . .

So, joining together in brotherly love,
Let us worship again Our Father above,
And forgetting our own
 little selfish desires
May we seek what "The Star"
 of Christmas inspires.

In this was manifested the love of God toward us, because that God sent his only begotten Son into the world, that we might live through him.

1 John 4:9

We Ask in Thy Name!

Bless us, heavenly Father,
      Forgive our erring ways,
Grant us strength to serve Thee,
      Put purpose in our days . . .
Give us understanding
      Enough to make us kind
So we may judge all people
      With our heart and not our mind . . .
And teach us to be patient
      In everything we do,
Content to trust Your wisdom
      And to follow after You . . .
And help us when we falter
      And hear us when we pray
And receive us in THY KINGDOM
      To dwell with Thee some day.

This is my prayer that I faithfully say
      To help me to meet the new dawning day,
For I never could meet life's daily demands
      Unless I was sure He was holding my hands . . .
And priceless indeed would be my reward
      To know that you shared My Prayer To the Lord.